BILLY
GRAHAM
Evangelistic Asso...
Always Good N...

D1368453

Dear Friend,

I am pleased to send you this copy of *Jesus Revealed*, a 40-day devotional of Old Testament prophecies that were fulfilled in the person of Jesus Christ.

This book will take you through 40 messianic passages written hundreds of years before our Savior's birth—and lists the corresponding New Testament verses as lived out by Christ. *Jesus Revealed* also features a daily meditation and prayer. I pray that God will bless each day's reading, so that you—like the two disciples on the road to Emmaus—will encounter the living Savior, who "*beginning with Moses and all the Prophets ... interpreted for them the things concerning Himself in all the Scriptures*" (Luke 24:27, HCSB).

For more than 60 years, the Billy Graham Evangelistic Association has worked to take the Good News of Jesus Christ throughout the world by every effective means available, and I'm excited about what God will do in the years ahead.

We would appreciate knowing how our ministry has touched your life. May God richly bless you.

Sincerely,

Franklin Graham
President

If you would like to know more about our ministry, please contact us:

IN THE U.S.:
Billy Graham Evangelistic Association
1 Billy Graham Parkway
Charlotte, NC 28201-0001
BillyGraham.org
info@bgea.org
Toll-free: 1-877-247-2426

IN CANADA:
Billy Graham Evangelistic
Association of Canada
20 Hopewell Way NE
Calgary, AB T3J 5H5
BillyGraham.ca
Toll-free: 1-888-393-0003

Jesus REVEALED

A 40-Day Discovery
of the SCRIPTURES FULFILLED
by JESUS, *the* ANOINTED SON *of* GOD

THOMAS NELSON
Since 1798

BILLY GRAHAM
Evangelistic Association
Always Good News.

NASHVILLE   DALLAS   MEXICO CITY   RIO DE JANEIRO

Jesus Revealed
© 2011 by Thomas Nelson

Published in Nashville, Tennessee, by Thomas Nelson®. Thomas Nelson is a registered trademark of Thomas Nelson, a division of HarperCollins Christian Publishing, Inc.

Unless otherwise noted, all Scripture quotations are from The Voice™ translation © 2011 Ecclesia Bible Society. Used by permission. All rights reserved.

Compiled and edited by Beth Ryan
Cover and interior design by Kristy L. Edwards

ISBN: 978-0-7180-0184-1

Printed in the United States of America

14 15 16 17 18 - PW - 5 4 3 2 1
www.thomasnelson.com

Note from the Publisher

Jesus
REVEALED

is a collection of 40 "messianic prophecies" that were
written hundreds of years before Jesus was born.

There are hundreds of messianic prophecies in the Bible.

A prophecy describes a "prediction of the future, made under
divine inspiration" or a "revelation of God."

A "messianic" prophecy is a prediction
about a "coming Messiah."

The 39 books that make up the Old Testament of the Bible were
written between 1450 B.C. and 430 B.C. and contain hundreds of
prophecies about the Messiah who would arrive years later. The
Messiah would come to deliver, save, and fulfill the promises made
to the Jewish people and to all believers. These prophecies and
promises also said that the Messiah would come to save all nations.

*May this 40-day journey bring you and those
you love closer to the Lord and strengthen your faith.*

HEIR *to the* THRONE *of* DAVID

Isaiah 9:7 *(Old Testament Prophecy)*

His leadership will bring such prosperity *as you've never seen before*—
sustainable peace for all time.
This child: God's promise to David—a throne forever, *among us,*
to restore sound leadership that cannot be perverted or shaken.
He will ensure justice without fail and absolute equity. Always.
The intense passion of the Eternal, Commander of *heavenly* armies,
will carry this to completion.

(Fulfilled in Jesus) Luke 1:32

Messenger: Jesus will become the greatest among men. He will be known as the Son of the Highest God. God will give Him the throne of His ancestor David.

THOUGHT

Hundreds of years before Jesus was born, God spoke through the prophet Isaiah and affirmed His promise to King David that He would send a "forever" heir.

Jesus, thank You that Your kingdom is forever. You are the perfect King whose reign will never end. Your kingdom cannot be shaken or threatened. Help me to remember that my identity is found in Your perfect life, death, and resurrection, and that I am a citizen in Your eternal kingdom.

BORN *of a* VIRGIN

Isaiah 7:14 (Old Testament Prophecy)

The Lord will give you a proof-sign anyway: See, a young maiden *(Greek, "virgin")* will conceive. She will give birth to a son and name Him Immanuel, *that is, "God with us."*

(Fulfilled in Jesus) Luke 1:26, 27, 30, 31

Six months later in Nazareth, a city in *the rural province of* Galilee, the heavenly messenger Gabriel made another appearance. This time the messenger was sent by God to meet with a virgin named Mary, who was engaged to a man named Joseph, a descendant of King David himself.

Messenger: Mary, don't be afraid. You have found favor with God. Listen, you are going to become pregnant. You will have a son, and you must name Him "Savior," *or* Jesus.

THOUGHT

God chose to reveal His plan to bring humanity back into relationship with Himself long before Jesus was born.

Thank You, God, that You control all things. While I was dead in my sins, You had a plan for redemption through the birth, life, death, and resurrection of Your Son, Jesus Christ. Thank You that You are faithful to the promises You make to Your people. While I am weak and broken, You are never-failing.

JESUS WILL BE BORN *in* BETHLEHEM

Micah 5:2 (Old Testament Prophecy)

Eternal One: But you, Bethlehem of Ephrathah,
   of the clans of Judah, are no poor relation—
From your people will come a Ruler
   who will be the shepherd of My people, Israel,
Whose origins date back to the distant past,
   to the ancient days.

(Fulfilled in Jesus) Matthew 2:4

Jesus was born in the town of Bethlehem, in the province of Judea, at the time when King Herod reigned.

THOUGHT

Bethlehem, the birthplace of King David, would not have surprised Micah's listeners as the place where the Ruler would be born; but centuries later when the prophecy is fulfilled, Bethlehem is only a community of several dozen families. God fulfilled His promise that Bethlehem would be the birthplace of the shepherd of His people.

Oh, Father, thank You for Your Word and for revealing long before it happened that Jesus would be born in Bethlehem. My faith is strengthened through this revelation. Encourage my heart today because You know the end from the beginning, and I trust You with every detail of my life.

JESUS WAS TAKEN *to* EGYPT

Hosea 11:1 (Old Testament Prophecy)

Eternal One: When Israel was a child, I loved him; and out of Egypt I called My son.

(Fulfilled in Jesus) Matthew 2:14-15

So Joseph got up in the middle of the night; he bundled up Mary and Jesus, and they left for Egypt. Joseph, Mary, and Jesus stayed *in Egypt* until Herod died. This fulfilled yet another prophecy. The prophet *Hosea* once wrote, "Out of Egypt I called My Son."

THOUGHT

God twice called His children out of Egypt: first Israel's descendants, God's chosen people, and then Jesus, who made everyone—Jews and Gentiles—into God's people.

Father, strengthen my faith by seeing that, long before Mary and Joseph had to take Jesus into Egypt to escape the wrath of King Herod, You knew it would happen. Oh, how You know every moment of my life. Help me to comprehend the enormous love You have for me, and may that alone be all the sustenance I need!

JESUS ANOINTED *by the* SPIRIT

Isaiah 11:2 (Old Testament Prophecy)

On this *child from David's line,* the Spirit of the Eternal One will
   alight and rest.
By the Spirit of wisdom and discernment
   He will shine like the dew.
By the Spirit of counsel and strength
   He will judge fairly and act courageously.

(Fulfilled in Jesus) Matthew 3:16

Jesus emerged from His baptism; and at that moment heaven was
opened, and Jesus saw the Spirit of God descending like a dove and
coming upon Him, *alighting on His very body.*

(Fulfilled in Jesus) Luke 4:18

Jesus: The Spirit of the Lord the Eternal One is on Me.
Why? Because the Eternal designated Me
   to be His representative to the poor, to preach good news to them.
He sent Me to tell those who are held captive that they can now be
      set free and to tell the blind that they can now see.

THOUGHT

Long before Jesus was here on earth in human form, God revealed that His Spirit would be on the child from David's lineage.

*Lord, You revealed that Your spirit would rest upon Jesus and that
He is Your chosen one. Oh, dear Jesus, You have come to set me free!
Help me to daily walk in the freedom and the sight that You give.*

JESUS IS GOD'S SERVANT

Isaiah 42:1 (Old Testament Prophecy)
Eternal One: Look here, let Me present My servant;
  I have taken hold of him. He is My chosen, and I delight in him.
I have put My Spirit on him; by this he will bring justice to the
  nations.

(Fulfilled in Jesus) Matthew 12:18
This is My servant, whom I have *well* chosen;
  this is the One I love, the One in whom I delight.
I will place My Spirit upon Him;
  He will proclaim justice to all the world.

THOUGHT

God is consistent in His message, no matter how many years are
between a prophecy and its fulfillment. Jesus is indeed chosen
by God and a just ruler of nations and God delights in Him.

*Dear Lord, today I am reminded that You are God's servant and
God delights in You. You have God's Spirit and You have made the
ultimate sacrifice so I can be adopted into Your family. You give me
the same Spirit to indwell my being. Help me to be Your servant as
You were God's chosen one. I now see how You delight in me just as
the Father delighted in You.*

MINISTRY *to the* BROKENHEARTED

Isaiah 61:1 (Old Testament Prophecy)
The Spirit of the Lord, the Eternal, is on me.
   The Lord has appointed me for a special purpose.
He has anointed me to bring good news to the poor.
   He has sent me to repair broken hearts,
And to declare to those who are held captive and bound in prison,
   "Be free *from your imprisonment!*"

(Fulfilled in Jesus) Luke 4:18
Jesus: The Spirit of the Lord the Eternal One is on Me.
Why? Because the Eternal designated Me
   to be His representative to the poor, to preach good news to them.
He sent Me to tell those who are held captive that they can now be
      set free . . .

THOUGHT

God made a way for broken hearts to be repaired and captives
to be freed. When Isaiah spoke these words to the exiles, he was
talking about himself and foreshadowing Jesus' work.

*Thank You, Lord, for the freedom found in You. I had no way to
break the bonds of sin in my life, but You have rescued me who is
poor in spirit and desperate for You. Although broken and sinful,
You have covered me by Your sacrifice and set me free. May I be
Your representative to the poor and those in prison of any kind
and above all help me to share Your good news!*

TENDER *and* LOVING SHEPHERD

Isaiah 40:11 (Old Testament Prophecy)

He will feed His fold like a shepherd;
  He will gather together His lambs—*the weak and the wobbly ones*—into His arms.
He will carry them close to His bosom,
  and tenderly lead like a shepherd the mother of her lambs.

(Fulfilled in Jesus) John 10:2-4

Jesus: The shepherd walks openly through the entrance. The guard who is posted to protect the sheep opens the gate for the shepherd, and the sheep hear his voice. He calls his own sheep by name and leads them out. When all the sheep have been gathered, he walks on ahead of them; and they follow him because they know his voice.

THOUGHT

Isaiah was inspired by the Spirit of God to explain how the coming Messiah, Jesus, would lead and care for people: as a shepherd leads and cares for his sheep.

Jesus, on my own I am like a defenseless sheep, and I tend to wander. You are my Protector and Savior. Thank You that You have allowed me to know Your voice. Thank You that You have led me out of exile by Your death on the cross and that You rescued me. Please continue to guide me and protect me.

JESUS IS IDENTIFIED *as the* LORD

Isaiah 41:4 (Old Testament Prophecy)

Eternal One: Who has performed *these deeds* and accomplished this
purpose?
Who calls each generation into being from the first *on down*?
It is I, the Eternal One *your God*.
I am the first.
And to the very last, I am the One.

(Fulfilled in Jesus) Revelation 1:11

A Voice: I am the Alpha and the Omega, the very beginning and the
very end.

(Fulfilled in Jesus) Revelation 1:17–18

The One: This is not the time for fear; I am the First and the Last, and
I am the living One. I entered the realm of the dead; but see, I am
alive now…

THOUGHT

Jesus and God are inseparable from each other and from the
Holy Spirit.

---

*Jesus, You are God. In the past, present, and future, You are there.
You alone have conquered death. Thank You for going to the cross
and taking upon Yourself the penalty for my sin. Because of Your
sacrifice and victory over death, I am redeemed to live forever
with You and see Your Glory. Thank You, Jesus.*

Triumphal Entry *into* Jerusalem

Zechariah 9:9 *(Old Testament Prophecy)*

Eternal One: Cry out with joy, O daughter of Zion!
Shout *jubilantly*, O daughter of Jerusalem!
Look—your King is coming;
He is righteous and able to save.
He comes seated humbly on a donkey,
on a colt, a foal of a donkey.

(Fulfilled in Jesus) John 12:13-14

. . . they gathered branches of palm trees to wave as they celebrated
His arrival.

Crowds *(shouting)*: Hosanna!
He who comes in the name of the Lord is truly blessed
and is King of all Israel.

Jesus found a young donkey, sat on it, *and rode through the crowds
mounted on this small beast.* The Scriptures foretold of this day...

THOUGHT

Over 500 years before Jesus entered Jerusalem on a donkey, God
foretold of it through the prophet Zechariah.

*Father, thank You for sending Jesus to earth and fulfilling Your
promise. Please help me to always remember that You are righteous and mighty to save, and may my joy be a reflection of Your
presence. May I worship You with all that I am and all that I have!*

BETRAYAL *of* JESUS

Psalm 41:9 (Old Testament Prophecy)
Even my best friend, my confidant
  who has eaten my bread will stab me in the back.

(Fulfilled in Jesus) John 13:26
Jesus: I will dip a piece of bread in My cup and give it to the one who
    will betray Me.
He dipped one piece in the cup and gave it to Judas, the son of Simon
Iscariot. After this occurred, Satan entered into Judas.

(Fulfilled in Jesus) Matthew 26:48b-50
Judas Iscariot: *I'll greet Him with a kiss.* And you will know that the
    one I kiss is the one you should arrest.
So at once, he went up to Jesus.
Judas Iscariot: Greetings, Teacher (he kisses Him).
Jesus: My friend, do what you have come to do.
And at that, the company came and seized Him.

THOUGHT

Hundreds of years before Judas betrayed Jesus the prophecy
referred to the betrayer as "best friend" and then when Jesus
spoke to Judas directly he addressed Judas as "My friend."

---

*Father, forgive me for the many times I have betrayed You. Help
me to remain faithful to You always. Living on the resurrection
side of the cross helps me to know more fully God's love story.*

FORSAKEN *by* DISCIPLES

Zechariah 13:7 (Old Testament Prophecy)

This is a message of the Eternal, Commander of *heavenly* armies.

Eternal One: Sword, begin to stir; be ready to strike My shepherd,
to strike the man at My side.

Strike the shepherd, and the sheep *of the flock* will scatter.
I'll turn My hand against the little ones.

(Fulfilled in Jesus) Mark 14:50

When they saw the armed crowd take Jesus into custody, the disciples fled.

THOUGHT

Good or bad, when great prophets or teachers are destroyed or disgraced, their followers disperse out of fear.

Father, Your Word is steadfast and true. May I be a disciple that follows You always and never flees. You are the Great Commander and go before me in every battle I face. May I live a life that reflects an understanding of that everlasting truth.

17

Price Paid *for* Jesus

Zechariah 11:12 (Old Testament Prophecy)

Zechariah *(to the sheep traders)*: If you think it is right, give me what I have earned. If you don't, then keep it *for yourselves.*

They took 30 pieces of silver, the price set as my wages, *the price of a slave.*

(Fulfilled in Jesus) Matthew 26:14-15

At that, one of the twelve, Judas Iscariot, went to the chief priests.

Judas Iscariot: What will you give me to turn Him over to you?

They offered him 30 pieces of silver.

THOUGHT

The love of money can cause us to betray even our best friend. The exiles paid Zechariah the same amount to dissolve their covenant with God as the Jewish leaders paid Judas to abandon his loyalty to Jesus. The love of money is the root of all sorts of evil.

Father, there is no greater price that was paid than the blood Christ shed for me. Thank You for the gift of eternal life through Christ. Your promise is true, Your love covers my debts, and You have made me clean. To You, I owe my everything. In You, I am made new. Help me to never betray You.

What Would Be Done *with* Money

Zechariah 11:13 (Old Testament Prophecy)

Eternal One *(to Zechariah)*: Give *My deserved portion of* your fee to the potter.

And I did as He told me. I took the 30 shekels of silver—the noble price of my valuable service—and gave them to the potter in the Eternal's temple.

(Fulfilled in Jesus) Matthew 27:4-7

Judas Iscariot: *I can't keep this money!* I've sinned! I've betrayed an innocent man! *His blood will be on my hands.*

Chief Priests and Elders: *We're through with you, friend.* The state of your soul is really none of our affair.

Judas threw down the money in the temple, went off, and hanged himself. The chief priests looked at the silver coins and picked them up.

Chief Priests and Elders: You know, according to the law, we can't put blood money in the temple treasury.

After some deliberation, they took the money and bought a plot of land called Potter's Field …

❖ ———————— THOUGHT ———————— ❖

The thirty shekels paid to both Zechariah and Judas signaled the exiles' and Jews' rejection of God.

❖ ———————————————————————— ❖

You know my every thought and action before I even move. Thank You for loving me through it all. Just as You knew he would, Judas betrayed You. You know the moments I will doubt You, turn from You, and reject Your teachings, and yet You love me still. Please forgive me.

Jesus' Scourging

Isaiah 50:5-6 (Old Testament Prophecy)

The Lord, the Eternal, has helped me to listen,
  and *I do as He says.* I have not been rebellious or run away *from
    God's work.*
But it's been hard. I offered My back to those who whipped me,
  my cheeks to those who pulled out my beard;
I did not turn away from humiliation and spitting.

(Fulfilled in Jesus) Matthew 27:26 and 30

So Pilate released Barabbas, and he had Jesus flogged and
handed over to be crucified. They spat on Him and whipped
Him on the head with *His scepter of* reeds . . .

❖ ———————— **THOUGHT** ———————— ❖

God, who was, who is, and who will always be, knows the end
from the beginning and He revealed through Isaiah centuries
before Jesus' trial almost the exact details of the beating, the
scourging, and the humiliation Jesus would go through.

❖ ———————————————————— ❖

*Jesus, Your wounds have healed me. I am unworthy of Your love
and redemption, but You have never stopped pursuing me. Thank
You for suffering for me and fulfilling Your promise. Please help
me to remember daily Your death on the cross, so that I may share
with others the sacrifice You made.*

His Marred Face

Isaiah 52:14 (Old Testament Prophecy)

Eternal One: Just as people used to be shocked by you,
   even so his appearance was disfigured;
His form—*once glorious*—was marred until it hardly seemed
      human.

(Fulfilled in Jesus) Mark 15:16b & 19

The rest of the soldiers in the detachment gathered there, *hundreds of
them.* For a long while they beat Him on the head with a reed …

THOUGHT

Many soldiers beat Jesus on the head and face with what equates
to a police officer's nightstick. Such a beating would have in-
flicted many wounds and would have caused Jesus to be almost
unrecognizable and horribly disfigured.

*Jesus, I cannot imagine how I would feel if, at this moment, I was
witnessing the beating You took, knowing that it should be me
who was being beaten. Oh, so incomprehensible is Your love for
me. May all my days be lived in gratitude and in humility that
only by Your grace and sacrifice am I alive.*

JESUS PUT *to* SHAME *and* DISHONOR

Psalm 69:4 (Old Testament Prophecy)

My enemies despise me without any cause;
   they outnumber the hairs on my head.
They torment me with their power;
   they have absolutely no reason to hate me.
Now I am set to pay for crimes
   I have never committed!

(Fulfilled in Jesus) John 15:24-25

Jesus: If I had not demonstrated things for them that have never been done, they would not be guilty of sin. But the reality is they have stared Me in the face, and they have despised Me and the Father nonetheless. Yet their law, which says, "They despised Me without any cause," has again been proven true.

THOUGHT

Some scholars say that Psalm 69 was written in 1000 B.C., but regardless of the actual date of the writing, these thoughts were recorded long before Jesus was falsely accused; God foretold it.

Lord Jesus, thank You for caring about all the details of my life. Forgive me for the times my lack of faith makes me just as guilty as those who despised You without cause. I know that You opened Your arms in forgiveness. I receive Your forgiveness and the life-giving power that You grant to me through Your Holy Spirit.

FALSE WITNESSES *at* HIS TRIAL

Psalm 35:11 (Old Testament Prophecy)

False witnesses step forward;
   they ask me *strange* questions for which I have no answers.

(Fulfilled in Jesus) Mark 14:56

There were plenty of people willing to get up and accuse Jesus falsely,
distorting what Jesus had said or done…

THOUGHT

David may not have had answers to the questions asked by his enemies, but Jesus would choose not to address the false accusations at all.

Dear Jesus, I confess there have been times that I have distorted what You have said in Your Word. Even if I have not distorted openly with my mouth, I have in my heart. Please increase my faith that daily I may walk by faith and not by sight. Thank You for being my rock, my fortress, and my deliverer. For in You I find refuge. I pray that the words of my mouth and the mediations of my heart will be pleasing to You.

HE WOULD NOT OPEN HIS MOUTH

Isaiah 53:7 (Old Testament Prophecy)

And in the face of such oppression and suffering—silence.
  Not a word of protest, *not a finger raised to stop it.*
Like a sheep to a shearing, like a lamb to be slaughtered,
  he went—oh so quietly, oh so willingly.

(Fulfilled in Jesus) Matthew 27:13-14

Pilate: Do You hear these accusations they are making against
  You?

Still Jesus said nothing, which Pilate found rather astounding—*no protests, no defense, nothing.*

✦ ─────── **THOUGHT** ─────── ✦

Amazingly Jesus said nothing in His defense; just maybe He did
so because He was taking our place of punishment. So in saying
nothing, He said everything!

✦ ─────────────────────── ✦

*Lord Jesus, I confess that it still bewilders me that You chose to say
nothing in Your defense. You had performed miracle after miracle,
and You could have called on all of heaven to wipe out all Your enemies, but You chose to say nothing. You did so because You were
determined to take my place of just punishment. Oh, may I live
daily in gratitude for Your silence, Your sacrifice, and the giving
of Your Spirit imparting to me a family heritage that cannot be
taken away. I love You, Lord!*

SOLDIERS GAMBLED *for* HIS CLOTHING

Psalm 22:18 (Old Testament Prophecy)
They *make a game out of* dividing my clothes among them-
    selves;
  they cast lots for the clothes on my back.

(Fulfilled in Jesus) John 19:24
Soldier *(to other soldiers)*: Don't tear it. Let's cast lots, and the
    winner will take the whole thing.

THOUGHT

In David's time, as well as in Jesus', nakedness indicated poverty
and servitude. God's greatest king of Israel and His only Son
both needed to experience the worst of humanity before they
could unite Israel and save humanity, respectively.

*Lord, these great revelations still amaze me! I know You have ris-
en, and I know You are KING of kings and LORD of lords; but oh,
how these verses strengthen my faith. For You told exactly what
would happen hundreds of years before it happened. Only an all-
knowing God could do such a thing. You are the great "I AM," Cre-
ator and Sustainer of all.*

JESUS IS MOCKED

Psalm 22:7-8 (Old Testament Prophecy)

Everyone who sees me laughs at me;
    they whisper *to one another* I'm a loser; they sneer and mock
    me, saying,
"He relies on the Eternal; let the Eternal rescue him…"

(Fulfilled in Jesus) Luke 23:35-37

Authorities *(mocking Jesus)***:** So He was supposed to rescue oth-
    ers, was He? He was supposed to be God's Anointed, *the*
    Liberating King? Let's see Him start by liberating Himself!

The soldiers joined in the mockery. First, they *pretended to offer*
Him a soothing drink—but it was sour wine.

Soldiers: Hey, if You're the King of the Jews, why don't You free
    Yourself!

THOUGHT

Reliance on God is no laughing matter. David would find that
God would crush his taunting enemies in battle. Jesus over-
looked the rude remarks and chose to save His enemies from
the same death they were about to inflict upon Him.

Oh, Lord, so many times I have mocked You, maybe not in the
same words used by the soldiers but certainly in the same spirit of
doubt. Forgive me, and help me to live each day in absolute faith,
knowing that You have all power and authority and that it was
Your enormous love for me that kept You on the cross.

JESUS IS THIRSTY

Psalm 69:3 (Old Testament Prophecy)

I am weary of howling;
   my throat is scratched dry.

(Fulfilled in Jesus) John 19:28

Jesus knew now that His work had been accomplished, and the Hebrew Scriptures were being fulfilled.
Jesus: I am thirsty.

THOUGHT

All that Jesus went through including the horrible thirst was out of love and desire for mankind to be restored to relationship with God.

Lord, I hunger and thirst for Your presence. Please remind me when I thirst for You or thirst for a drink that You chose to take my place of suffering. May my desire for You be unquenchable.

HE IS GIVEN SOUR DRINK

Psalm 69:24 (Old Testament Prophecy)
Even more, they gave me poison for my food
  and offered me *only sour* vinegar to drink.

(Fulfilled in Jesus) John 19:29
A jar of sour wine had been left there, so they took a hyssop branch
with a sponge soaked in the vinegar and put it to His mouth.

THOUGHT

Chased through the wilderness and finally captured, David
needs a little kindness from his captors. Hanging on a cross in
the hot Judean sun, Jesus asks for a drink. Neither receives mercy from his enemies but is tortured even more. The method and
length of time for crucifixion would cause unimaginable thirst.

*Lord, may I be reminded that even though the circumstances
of life can often put a sour taste in my mouth, I will taste and
see that You are good. I am grateful that Your thirst for me was
so great that nothing but Your sacrifice could satisfy that thirst.
Thank You!*

Pierced *through* Hands *and* Feet

Psalm 22:16 (Old Testament Prophecy)

A throng of evil ones has surrounded me
  like *a pack of wild* dogs;
They pierced my hands and *ripped a hole in* my feet.

(Fulfilled in Jesus) John 20:27

He drew close to Thomas.

Jesus: Reach out and touch Me. See the punctures in My hands;
    reach out your hand, and put it to My side; leave behind
    your faithlessness, and believe.

THOUGHT

Even after Jesus came back to life, the punctures in His hands
and the hole in His side were visible. Thomas did not believe
until he saw Jesus in person. Jesus went on to say, "Blessed are
all those who never see Me and yet they still believe."

*Lord, I confess that sometimes I am like Thomas with a lack of
faith. But oh, how this verse strengthens my faith seeing that the
Holy Spirit revealed exactly what would happen to You hundreds
of years before it happened. Seeing how You responded to Thomas
helps me to know that You reach out in loving tenderness and
touch me with Your nail-pierced hand and ask me to leave faith-
lessness behind. Oh, may my un-nailed feet go where You lead and
my un-nailed hands reach out with Your love and do what You
want me to do.*

29

HIS SIDE PIERCED

Zechariah 12:10 (Old Testament Prophecy)

Eternal One: And *I pledge that* I will pour out a spirit of grace and
pleas for mercy on the family of David and the citizens of
Jerusalem. As a result, they will look upon Me whom they
pierced, they will grieve over Him as one grieves for an only
child, and they will moan and weep for Him as one weeps
for a firstborn son.

(Fulfilled in Jesus) John 19:34

One soldier took his spear and pierced His abdomen, which brought a
gush of blood and water.

THOUGHT

Roman soldiers were commanded to break the crucified person's legs not pierce the side of the person. The Passover sacrificial regulations did not allow for the breaking of bones, so God
fulfilled His Word down to the very detail.

*Dear Jesus, I cannot begin to comprehend the love You have for me
that You would be willing to lay down Your life and let blood and
water flow from You in order to redeem me. May I be mindful and
thankful every moment of every day that You love me so deeply
and completely.*

Prays *for* Betrayers

Psalm 109:1-4 (Old Testament Prophecy)

O True God of my *every* praise, do not keep silent!
My enemies have opened their wicked, deceit-filled mouths *and
    blown their foul breath* on me.
  They have slandered me with their twisted tongues
And unleashed loathsome words that swirl around me.
  Though I have done nothing, they attack me.
Though I offer them love and keep them in my prayers, they
    accuse me.

(Fulfilled in Jesus) Luke 23:34

Jesus: Father, forgive them, for they don't know what they're doing.

THOUGHT

King David was tortured by his enemies, and like the rest of us would, he asked God to punish them. But not Jesus. With some of His last words, the Savior begged God to forgive his torturers, to forgive us. Only the Spirit of God can offer prayer for such perpetrators.

Lord, the thought that You continually love me and pray for me by interceding with the Holy Spirit comforts me in unexplainable ways. Why do I ever enter into that place of fear that causes me to act and react in ways that are not pleasing to You? You have sent Your Holy Spirit to me. I beseech You to continue to pray for me that I will love through the power of Your Spirit. May I become all that You purpose for me to become!

MOTHER *and* FRIENDS *at a* DISTANCE

Psalm 38:11 (Old Testament Prophecy)

Even my friends and loved ones turn away when they see this marked man;

those closest to me are no longer close at all.

(Fulfilled in Jesus) Luke 23:49

And all who knew Jesus personally, including the group of women who had been with Him *from the beginning* in Galilee, stood at a distance, watching all of these things unfold.

THOUGHT

Knowing that Jesus took all the punishment due you and that you should be the one receiving all the horrible punishment, do you still distance yourself from Jesus when it's not convenient or cool?

Father, truth be known, there are times that I deny You. It may not be outright denial, but in my thoughts I deny You when I have a lack of faith. Oh, please erase my unbelief and impart to me the courage to stand up for truth, to speak out in light of Your truth, and most of all to be a bold witness of Your love to a desperate and hurting world.

MOCKERS SHAKE THEIR HEADS *at* HIM

Psalm 109:25 (Old Testament Prophecy)

I have become a person of contempt to my accusers;
   whenever they see me, they *taunt me*, shaking their heads *in
      disapproval.*

(Fulfilled in Jesus) Matthew 27:39

Passersby shouted curses and blasphemies at Jesus. They wagged their
heads *at Him and hissed*.

THOUGHT

While Jesus was born in a very quiet setting, His death was in a
very public place where hundreds of people were passing by. He
endured being publicly humiliated to give His life as a ransom
for many!

---

*Lord, are there times I mock You? Oh, how conviction sets in
on my heart. I wonder what You could accomplish through me
if I had absolute and complete faith in You and the resurrection
power that You offer to me. Oh, dear Jesus, this journey is tough,
and sometimes I let the world influence my thoughts and actions.
Please continue Your redeeming work in my heart, mind, and
soul. Thank You for revealing Your truth that sets me free.*

MAKING SARCASTIC REMARKS *at* HIM

Psalm 22:8 (Old Testament Prophecy)
"He relies on the Eternal; let the Eternal rescue him
and keep him safe because He is happy with him."

(Fulfilled in Jesus) Matthew 27:43
Chief Priests, Scribes, and Elders *(mocking Him)***:** He claimed
communion with God—well, let God save Him, if He's
God's beloved Son.

THOUGHT

Amazingly so many people saw Jesus perform miracle after
miracle, and yet they couldn't comprehend God's plan to redeem humanity and return them to His family. Instead of ask-
ing for an explanation of Jesus' crucifixion, the people taunted
what they didn't understand.

---

*Dear Jesus, I confess that when I read these words my heart leaps,
for I know that You are the beloved Son of God who loves me so
much that You took my place of just punishment. I smile in my
heart at the thought that, yes, the Eternal One, God of heaven and
earth, did rescue You, His Anointed Son, and the reason was so
You could rescue me. Oh happy day it truly is; for I am rescued,
redeemed, and living in communion with the KING of kings and
the LORD of lords!*

BROUGHT *as a* LAMB

Isaiah 53:7 (Old Testament Prophecy)

In the face of such oppression and suffering—silence.
  Not a word of protest, *not a finger raised to stop it.*
Like a sheep to a shearing, like a lamb to be slaughtered,
  he went—oh so quietly, oh so willingly.

(Fulfilled in Jesus) John 1:29

The morning after *this conversation,* John sees Jesus coming toward him. *In eager astonishment,* he shouts out:

John the Baptist: Look! *This man is more than He seems!* He is the Lamb sent from God, *the sacrifice* to erase the sins of the world!

THOUGHT

Each family in Israel had to have a lamb at Passover each year to shed its blood as a sacrificial offering to restore relationship with God and pay for their sins. But only the Lamb of God, Jesus, the Anointed Son of God's blood could take away the sins of the world once and for all.

Lord, I am still astounded that You chose not to say a thing in Your defense, but I trust completely in Your redemptive plan. Thank You, Jesus, for Your willingness to be the sacrificial Lamb that takes away my sin. I praise Your holy and magnificent name, JESUS, MESSIAH, LAMB OF GOD!

Vicarious Sacrifice

Isaiah 53:5-6 (Old Testament Prophecy)

He was hurt because of us; *he suffered so.*
  Our wrongdoing *wounded and* crushed him.
He endured the breaking that made us whole.
  The injuries he suffered became our healing.
We all have wandered off, like *shepherdless* sheep,
  scattered by our aimless striving and endless pursuits;
The Eternal One laid on him, *this silent sufferer,*
  the sins of us all.

(Fulfilled in Jesus) Romans 5:6 & 8

When the time was right, the Anointed One died for all of us who were far from God, powerless and weak. But *think about this:* while we were wasting our lives in sin, God revealed His powerful love to us *in a tangible display*—the Anointed One died for us.

THOUGHT

Centuries before Jesus was born, God through His Holy Spirit prophesied in explicit details the suffering Jesus would endure for us.

Father, long before I was born, You set forth Your merciful plan of redemption. You saw every sin in me and every foolish path I would take. Yet, in Your unfathomable mercy, You sent Jesus to die in my place. Thank You for bearing my shame on the cross and displaying Your love for me. Please be the king of my heart today.

No Bones Broken

Psalm 34:20 (Old Testament Prophecy)

He will protect all of their bones;
   not even one bone will be broken.

(Fulfilled in Jesus) John 19:32-36

The soldiers came and broke the legs of both the men crucified next to Jesus. When they came up to Jesus' cross, they could see that He was dead; so they did not break His legs. Instead, one soldier took his spear and pierced His abdomen, which brought a gush of blood and water. This testimony is true. In fact, it is an eyewitness account; and he has reported what he saw so that you also may believe. It happened this way to fulfill the Hebrew Scriptures that "not one of His bones shall be broken."

THOUGHT

Why did the soldiers not break the legs of Jesus; could it be because Jesus was already dead or to fulfill the requirements of the sacrificial Lamb to have no broken bones or perhaps because love had accomplished its purpose?

Father, I confess that in my own understanding I cannot comprehend the enormity of Your love for me. May I daily look at You upon the cross and ponder in my heart that God, the Eternal, has shed Your blood for my sins, and may I live my life in deep gratitude to You and share with others Your love.

CRUCIFIED *with* CRIMINALS

Isaiah 53:12 (Old Testament Prophecy)

Because he exposed his very self—
    laid bare his soul to the vicious grasping of death—
And was counted among the worst, I will count him among the
        best.

(Fulfilled in Jesus) Mark 15:27-28

On either side of Him were two insurgents *who also had received the death penalty*. And the Hebrew Scripture was completed that said, "He was considered just another criminal."

❖ —————— THOUGHT —————— ❖

Jesus allowed the Jewish leaders to make him an enemy of Rome and deserving of a common criminal's death. But we are the common criminals, no better than the traitors on either side of Him, who deserve the death He accepted.

❖ ——————————————————————————— ❖

Dear Jesus, I know I am guilty and should have hung in Your place, but oh, how I sit humbly at Your feet weeping in gratitude for what You have done for me. May I live a life worthy of the redemption You extend to me. May I live a life fulfilling all Your purposes for me. May I love with Your love and share Your great love story!

An Intense, Lonely Cry

Psalm 22:1 (Old Testament Prophecy)

My God, my God, why have You turned Your back on me?
Your ears are deaf to my groans.

(Fulfilled in Jesus) Matthew 27:46

In the middle of the dark afternoon, Jesus cried out in a loud voice.
Jesus: Eli, Eli, lama sabachthani—My God, My God, why have
You forsaken Me?

THOUGHT

The most horrible existence in this world is a life separated
from God. Yet, as King David lamented about himself and his
descendant the Messiah, God's own Son was separated from
Him while He hung on the cross so we wouldn't be.

*Father God, in dark and desperate moments, I have felt alone,
abandoned, and forsaken. In my despair, I've cried out to You for
comfort and You have heard my cries. Thank You for making our
relationship possible through the abandonment, death, and resurrection of Your Son. Praise Your name, the Alpha and the Omega,
the beginning and the end. I trust You, and I am living in Your
day, not mine. Take my life and consecrate it to Your will today.*

COMMITTED HIS SPIRIT

Psalm 31:5 (Old Testament Prophecy)
I entrust my spirit into Your hands.

Luke 23:46 (Fulfilled in Jesus)
Jesus (*shouting out loudly*): Father, I entrust My spirit into Your hands!

THOUGHT

As prophesied by the psalmist and seen in the Gospels, Jesus entrusted His life fully to the Father's care. Even in death, He offered it up to God on our behalf with total trust and confidence that God is faithful.

Father, help me to trust You with my life the way Jesus trusted You with His. Help me to see that there is nothing to fear in life or death because You are always faithful to Your children. Today, this day, I once again offer myself to You. Do with me as You desire for I am fully Yours.

JESUS DIED

Psalm 22:14-15 (Old Testament Prophecy)

My life is poured out like water,
 and all my bones have slipped out of joint.
My heart melts like wax inside me.
My strength is gone, dried up like shards of pottery;
 my *dry* tongue sticks to the roof of my mouth;
 You lay me in the dust of death.

Mark 15:44-45 (Fulfilled in Jesus)

Pilate could not believe Jesus was already dead, so he sent for the Centurion, who confirmed it.

THOUGHT

David was using imagery to describe his pain and fatigue during war, but Jesus literally experienced these things. Water poured from His side, His joints separated after hours of hanging, His heart was encased in fluid as it tried to beat, He was exhausted by scourging, and He was impossibly thirsty.

Dear Jesus, You completely overwhelm me as I cannot comprehend such a love as Yours, proven in what You did for me. Oh, forgive me for all the times that I have taken such a sacrifice for granted, for the times I chose to walk by sight rather than faith. I pray this day that You begin a new work in me and help me to walk completely by faith, for I know that is pleasing to You.

DARKNESS TAKES *over the* DAY

Amos 8:9 (Old Testament Prophecy)

Eternal One: On that day, I will make the sun set at noon and send darkness across the earth when it should be broad daylight.

(Fulfilled in Jesus) Matthew 27:45

Starting at noon, the entire land became dark. It was dark for three hours.

❖ ——————— **THOUGHT** ——————— ❖

God revealed through His Holy Spirit to the prophet Amos, who lived over 700 years before Jesus was crucified, that "on that day" the sun will set at noon and darkness will be over the earth. And then Matthew, an eyewitness, confirms that the entire land became dark for three hours. The darkness accompanying Jesus' crucifixion is Matthew's first supernatural sign preceding the salvation of not only Israel but the world.

❖ ——————————————————— ❖

Father, sometimes it feels like darkness swallows the light of day in my own life; sometimes I feel I've come to the end of my rope. Then I remember that Jesus hung on the cross at just such a time for me, bearing judgment's burden so I could be free. Thank You, that when darkness swallowed the sun, Your Son was swallowing up death in victory.

BURIED *in* BORROWED TOMB

Isaiah 53:9 (Old Testament Prophecy)

And when he was dead, he was buried with the disgraced
   in borrowed space (among the rich),
Even though he did no wrong by word or deed.

(Fulfilled in Jesus) Matthew 27:57-60

At evening time, a rich man from Arimathea arrived. His name was
Joseph, and he had become a disciple of Jesus. He went to Pilate and
asked to be given Jesus' body; Pilate assented and ordered his servants
to turn Jesus' body over to Joseph. So Joseph took the body, wrapped
Jesus in a clean sheath of white linen, and laid Jesus in his own new
tomb, which he had carved from a rock.

THOUGHT

Joseph of Arimathea had become a disciple of Jesus. He was
honoring Jesus the only way he knew how; little did Joseph
know that three days later Jesus' body wouldn't need a tomb
anymore!

*Jesus, Eternal One, You suffered the disgrace of a horrible public
death; like Joseph I want to offer You what I have, but nothing I
have is worthy of You! But You, in Your great love for me, simply
reach Your hand out to me and say, "Child, you are all I want and
I want to give you a life more abundant."*

He Will Rise Again *to* Life

Psalm 118:15b, 16-17 (Old Testament Prophecy)

"The right hand of the Eternal has shown His power.
The mighty arm of the Eternal is raised *in victory*;
  the right hand of His has shown His power."
I will not die. I will live.
  I will live to tell about all the Eternal has done.

(Fulfilled in Jesus) Mark 16:6-7

Man in White: Don't be afraid. You came seeking Jesus of Nazareth,
  the One who was crucified. He is gone. He has risen. See the place
  where His body was laid.

◆ ——————— **THOUGHT** ——————— ◆

Jesus rose from the dead and was seen by many documented
eyewitnesses. God chose to reveal His plan to redeem mankind,
and each of His proclamations about the coming Messiah has
been revealed in Jesus. What is God's victory that the psalmist
described? It's the rising of His Son from the grave.

◆ ——————————————————————— ◆

*Jesus, You said that You would never leave me nor forsake me, and
I take You at Your Word. The Father did not abandon You to the
grave, but raised You up in the power of His Spirit. Because You
live, I can live also. Because You were not abandoned, I know You
will never abandon me. You are with me today and for the rest of
my life, throughout eternity!*

THE HOLY SPIRIT GIVEN *to* BELIEVERS

Isaiah 44:3-8 (Old Testament Prophecy)
Eternal One: *Like a devoted gardener,* I will pour *sweet* water on
   parched land,
   streams on hard-packed ground;
I will pour My spirit on your children and grandchildren—
   and let My blessing flow to your descendants.
And they will sprout among the grasses, *grow vibrant and tall*
   like the willow trees lining a riverbank.
One will call out: "I belong to the Eternal."
   Another will say, "Jacob *is my people;* Israel my honored name."
Yet others will write "Property of the Eternal" on their hands.

The Eternal, Commander of *heavenly* armies,
   King of Israel, who paid their ransom, has this to say:
Eternal One: I am at the beginning and will be at the end.
   There is no God except for Me.
If you know any God like Me, tell it now.
   Declare and demonstrate any who can compare to Me.
Or if you know and have announced events before their time,
   told what is to come, then speak so now.
Don't be afraid. *Let your minds* be clear of fear.
   Haven't I announced events and revealed what is to come?
From the earliest days, I have done so. You know it—you have
      seen and know.

(Fulfilled in Jesus) John 20:21-23

Jesus: I give you the gift of peace. In the same way the Father
sent Me, I am now sending you.

Now He drew close enough to each of them that *they could feel
His breath.* He breathed on them:

Jesus: Welcome the Holy Spirit of the living God. You now have the
mantle of God's forgiveness. As you go, you are able to share the
life-giving power to forgive sins, or to withhold forgiveness.

(Fulfilled in Jesus) Acts 2:17-21

Peter: Hear what God says!

I will offer My Spirit to humanity as a libation.
Your children will boldly speak *the word of the Lord.*
Young warriors will see visions,
 and your elders will dream dreams.
Yes, in those days I shall offer My Spirit to all servants,
 both male and female, and they will boldly speak My word.
And in the heaven above and on the earth below,
I shall give signs *of impending judgment:* blood, fire, and
 clouds of smoke.
The sun will become a void of darkness,
 and the moon will become blood.
Then the great and dreadful day of the Lord will arrive,
And everyone who calls on the name of the Lord
 will be liberated *into God's freedom and peace.*

God had a plan to redeem you from the very beginning of time. He loves you so much that He came to earth and dwelt among us. He took your punishment for everything you've done wrong and everything you will do wrong, and He executed the deserved punishment upon HIS ONLY SON. Jesus was the perfect, unblemished Lamb of God, and He was given by God for our sins.

The Holy Spirit spoke through Paul and said, "So if you believe deep in your heart that God raised Jesus from the *pit of death* and if you voice your allegiance by confessing *the truth* that 'Jesus is Lord,' then you will be saved. Belief begins in the heart and leads to *a life that's* right with God" (Romans 10:9–10a).

Lord, I live in a hectic and chaotic world, and only You can provide true and lasting peace. I accept Your sacrifice that God offered for me. You truly are the Son of the Most High God. Prince of Peace, breathe Your Holy Spirit on me today; fill me with the same wholeness and assurance that Your earliest disciples felt when You breathed on them. I desire that same mantle of forgiveness You gave them—help me be a peacemaker. I have faith, and I know and trust that You died for me, but oh, how these revelations from Your Word are strengthening my faith. I now confess that I must know Your Word better, for all of Scripture points to the depth of love You have for me and that Your plan was and is being fulfilled from the beginning of time to the end of time. Keep my eyes and my heart steadfast in Your will and empower me to accomplish Your purposes for my life. I am Yours. AMEN.

STEPS TO PEACE WITH GOD

1. GOD'S PURPOSE: PEACE AND LIFE

God loves you and wants you to experience peace and life—abundant and eternal.

THE BIBLE SAYS ...

"We have peace with God through our Lord Jesus Christ." *Romans 5:1, ESV*

"For God so loved the world that He gave His only begotten Son, that whoever believes in Him should not perish but have everlasting life." *John 3:16, NKJV*

"I have come that they may have life, and that they may have it more abundantly." *John 10:10, NKJV*

Since God planned for us to have peace and the abundant life right now, why are most people not having this experience?

2. OUR PROBLEM: SEPARATION FROM GOD

God created us in His own image to have an abundant life. He did not make us as robots to automatically love and obey Him, but gave us a will and a freedom of choice.

We chose to disobey God and go our own willful way. We still make this choice today. This results in separation from God.

THE BIBLE SAYS ...

"For all have sinned and fall short of the glory of God." *Romans 3:23, ESV*

"For the wages of sin is death, but the gift of God is eternal life in Christ Jesus our Lord." *Romans 6:23, ESV*

Our choice results in separation from God.

People (Sinful)

God (Holy)

OUR ATTEMPTS

Through the ages, individuals have tried in many ways to bridge this gap ... without success ...

THE BIBLE SAYS ...

"There is a way that seems right to a man, but its end is the way to death."
Proverbs 14:12, ESV

"But your iniquities have separated you from your God; and your sins have hidden His face from you, so that He will not hear."
Isaiah 59:2, NKJV

There is only one remedy for this problem of separation.

3. GOD'S REMEDY: THE CROSS

Jesus Christ is the only answer to this problem. He died on the cross and rose from the grave, paying the penalty for our sin and bridging the gap between God and people.

THE BIBLE SAYS ...

"For there is one God, and there is one mediator between God and men, the man Christ Jesus."
1 Timothy 2:5, ESV

"For Christ also suffered once for sins, the just for the unjust, that He might bring us to God."
1 Peter 3:18, NKJV

"But God demonstrates His own love toward us, in that while we were still sinners, Christ died for us." *Romans 5:8, NKJV*

God has provided the only way ... we must make the choice ...

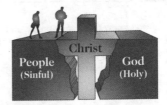

4. OUR RESPONSE: RECEIVE CHRIST

We must trust Jesus Christ and receive Him by personal invitation.

THE BIBLE SAYS ...

"Behold, I stand at the door and knock. If anyone hears My voice and opens the door, I will come in to him and dine with him, and he with Me." *Revelation 3:20, NKJV*

"But as many as received Him, to them He gave the right to become children of God, to those who believe in His name." *John 1:12, NKJV*

"If you confess with your mouth the Lord Jesus and believe in your heart that God has raised Him from the dead, you will be saved." *Romans 10:9, NKJV*

Are you here ... or here?

People — Sin, Rebellion, Separation — Christ — God — Peace, Forgiveness, Abundant Life, Eternal Life

Is there any good reason why you cannot receive Jesus Christ right now?

HOW TO RECEIVE CHRIST:

1. Admit your need (say, "I am a sinner").
2. Be willing to turn from your sins (repent) and ask for God's forgiveness.
3. Believe that Jesus Christ died for you on the cross and rose from the grave.
4. Through prayer, invite Jesus Christ to come in and control your life through the Holy Spirit (receive Jesus as Lord and Savior).

WHAT TO PRAY:

Dear Lord Jesus,
    I know that I am a sinner, and I ask for Your forgiveness. I believe You died for my sins and rose from the dead. I turn from my sins and invite You to come into my heart and life. I want to trust and follow You as my Lord and Savior.

        In Your Name, amen.

_____   _____
Date   Signature

GOD'S ASSURANCE: HIS WORD

IF YOU PRAYED THIS PRAYER,

THE BIBLE SAYS ...

"For, 'Everyone who calls on the name of the Lord will be saved.'"
Romans 10:13, ESV

Did you sincerely ask Jesus Christ to come into your life? Where is He right now? What has He given you?

"For by grace you have been saved through faith. And this is not your own doing; it is the gift of God, not a result of works, so that no one may boast." *Ephesians 2:8–9, ESV*

THE BIBLE SAYS ...

"He who has the Son has life; he who does not have the Son of God does not have life. These things I have written to you who believe in the name of the Son of God, that you may know that you have eternal life, and that you may continue to believe in the name of the Son of God."
1 John 5:12–13, NKJV

Receiving Christ, we are born into God's family through the supernatural work of the Holy Spirit who indwells every believer. This is called regeneration or the "new birth."

This is just the beginning of a wonderful new life in Christ. To deepen this relationship you should:

1. Read your Bible every day to know Christ better.
2. Talk to God in prayer every day.
3. Tell others about Christ.
4. Worship, fellowship, and serve with other Christians in a church where Christ is preached.
5. As Christ's representative in a needy world, demonstrate your new life by your love and concern for others.

God bless you as you do.

Billy Graham

If you want further help in the decision you have made, write to:
Billy Graham Evangelistic Association
1 Billy Graham Parkway, Charlotte, NC 28201-0001

1-877-2GRAHAM (1-877-247-2426)
BillyGraham.org/Commitment

NOTES

NOTES

NOTES

NOTES

NOTES

NOTES

NOTES

NOTES

NOTES

NOTES

NOTES

NOTES